Women of the Last Supper

We Were There Too

Millie N.S.

Women of the Last Supper
We Were There Too

For information or additional copies,
contact MillieNS@aol.com
or PO Box 2445, Chesterton IN 46304

Printed in the U.S.A. by InstantPublisher.com

for my wonderful granddaughters
Eva, Else, Hilda, and unborn others

and for their marvelous mothers
my daughters Marla, Beth, and Sharon

who reflect that girls and women
have long been amazing disciples of Jesus Christ

with great gratitude for those
who have inspired and supported these stories

especially my mom Blanche and my dad Fred
and my brother Doug and my husband Dave
and my sons Peter, Rod, and Peter

along with Pastor Terry and the Joy Circle
who dared to present a different view

with special thanks to my son Peter
for becoming my first publisher

Preface

Each of the women portrayed in these monologs was an ordinary person transformed by the power of Jesus Christ.

You, too, can experience this transformation, and live or die for the glory of God.

These monologs have been performed for churches, libraries, and clubs – providing affirmation for both women and men followers of Christ today, as well as stirring great community interest and positive press coverage in local newspapers.

Consider using these monologs for your church's Easter pageant, as a discussion text for your Sunday School class or small group, or for your own personal reflection, meditation and prayer.

Growing up in China, the author saw how the Christian faith gave dignity and freedom to Chinese women. Seeing the dramatic improvement in the quality of women's lives under Christianity, Millie became an advocate for women's rights and dignity. Her passion has led her to write these memoirs that illuminate the important role women had in the life and ministry of Jesus.

She is available to speak about the Biblical and historical significance of these monologs and to perform them. Contact her at MillieNS@aol.com or at PO Box 2445, Chesterton IN 46304.

Introduction

Have you ever wondered about most portrayals of the Lord's Last Supper being men only? During that family Passover meal held in a rooftop upper room, haven't you wondered where the women were? The women who were with Jesus and his twelve disciples just before and just after the Last Supper according to Gospel accounts?

You're right to wonder, because a number of Jesus' women followers were likely there at the Last Supper. No doubt they prepared and served that Passover meal as they had countless other meals.

In fact, various ancient artworks reflect this view – just not the one Leonardo da Vinci painted. Since his famous mural is on the wall of a monastery dining hall in Milan, it's no wonder he showed only twelve men disciples with Christ. But hasn't that perception dominated long enough? Isn't it time for a different, more realistic view of the Lord's Last Supper?

I think so! And my answer follows decades of reading, research and reflection.

As the Gospel writers repeatedly remind us: *"Many women followed Jesus, providing for Him from their substance . . ."* (Matthew 27:55). These were devout women of wealth and position who joyfully lived for their Lord and Savior, Jesus Christ – often sacrificing greatly, sometimes even their lives.

May you be blessed as you read these Biblically based accounts of a different view of the Last Supper, as you ponder these historical fiction memoirs of the women disciples who likely were there too.

Millie N.S.
2003

The angel answered and said to the women,
Do not be afraid,
for I know you seek Jesus who was crucified.
He is not here; for HE IS RISEN, as he said.
Go quickly and tell his disciples."
(Matthew 28:5-7)

Contents

Mary: A Mother Blessed	Chapter 1
Salome: A Privileged Aunt	Chapter 2
"Naomi": An Outcast No Longer	Chapter 3
Mary the Magdalene: An Early Church Leader	Chapter 4
"Judith": Wife of Joseph of Arimathea	Chapter 5
An Unnamed Woman: The Wife of Simon Peter	Chapter 6
Martha: The Sister of Mary from Bethany	Chapter 7
Joanna & Susanna: "Twin" Followers of Christ	Chapter 8
Mary: John Mark's Mother and Rhoda's Owner	Chapter 9
Abridged Presentation	Chapter 10

Author's Note: These monologs reflect a lifetime of reading, research and reflection. They are historical fiction, but based on the best information that I have found, and supplemented with plausible details where necessary for the narrative. With regard to the names, "Naomi," "Judith," "Philip," and "twins" are my own name and sibling choices based on Biblical and historical plausibility. Biblical passages are from the Wesley Bible, the New King James Version.

Chapter 1

Mary: A Mother Blessed Memoir of a Woman Disciple

I am Mary of Nazareth – the mother of Jesus Christ, and one his close followers present at the Last Supper. Yes, I was a mother uniquely blessed – but also one acquainted with deepest grief.

My soul still magnifies the Lord when I recall the extraordinary events of my life. For whoever would have thought Yahweh would choose someone from Nazareth to bring into the world the Messiah – our Savior Jesus Christ, Redeemer of the World!

As you know from Biblical and historical records, I was from Nazareth located in southern Galilee. In Aramaic, Nazareth means "watchtower," a fitting name for my hometown that overlooked an important highway, and one frequented by trade caravans and Roman troops. Because traders and soldiers often camped in our community during their travels, other Jews liked to joke, "Can anything good come out of Nazareth?"

Jesus certainly changed that perception, didn't he?

In truth, Nazareth was a good place to live in my time. Because of its usefulness to soldiers and traders, those of us who lived there were comparatively safe and prosperous. Many Nazarenes were skilled artisans and craftsmen – like my husband Joseph, a highly regarded woodcarver and carpenter. I'm not sure why we have often been stereotyped as peasants, for most of us were not. Thanks to our location, we were some of the most cosmopolitan people in the Land of Palestine.

Joseph's family and mine were from the Tribe of Judah and descendants of the royal line of David. Had we lived before the terrible wars and captivities of the Jewish people, you would remember us as Prince Joseph and Princess Mary. Ponder that a moment – makes the title *Prince of Peace* for my son Jesus more meaningful, doesn't it?

Because of my royal heritage, I was fortunate to have more privileges than many young women of my time. Although my own family's circumstances were reduced by misfortune, I had many caring relatives. Among these were Uncle Joseph, a wealthy merchant from Arimathea, and my mother's cousin Elizabeth and her husband, Priest Zacharias.

These relatives and others encouraged my sister Salome and me to have strong faith in Yahweh. They urged us to study the Law with diligence, often using the ancient Torah scrolls in their homes. To our family, we were not just girls, but girls with a special heritage and purpose. Who knew what Yahweh might require of us? We might become another Miriam or Deborah, Esther or Ruth, or even the mother of the promised Messiah.

Ah, as you can see, not only was I a blessed female, I was a fortunate one. And the day came when I had wondrous reason to sing, *"My soul magnifies the Lord, and my spirit has rejoiced in God my Savior."*

I will tell you how it happened.

When Salome and I were old enough to marry, our mother Anne and other relatives began the search for our husbands. Because Mother wanted us to have happy marriages, the search was not a hurried one. So I was a year or two past sixteen by the time Joseph and I became engaged. By then, my sister Salome was already married to Zebedee, a prosperous fisherman from Capernaum by Lake Galilee.

In my time, an engagement or betrothal lasted about a year and was as binding as marriage. If the espoused wife became pregnant before the marriage ceremony, not much was said if the ceremony took place sooner than planned. However, if the espoused husband accused his betrothed of betrayal, then there was trouble – sometimes resulting in a quiet divorce, sometimes in a public and humiliating divorce, or sometimes even in stoning to death.

So you can imagine the mixture of trepidation and excitement I felt when I told Joseph I was pregnant with the long-awaited Messiah. As I described to him my awesome encounter with the Angel Gabriel, Joseph became increasingly distressed. He wanted to believe me, but he just couldn't.

He needed time alone to think, he told me. Before he pushed me from him and hurried away, he assured me that if he broke our engagement, I would be quietly divorced and not stoned. To my mother's great relief, he did not make an immediate decision. I knew Mother believed me and felt the same wonder I did. At the same time, she was concerned about my future. And what loving mother wouldn't be?

However, God took care of our anxieties. That night the angel brought another message from God – this time to Joseph. At once, Joseph's suspicions about my miraculous conception were quelled. He was content to marry me, and I him.

Not long after, Mother and I visited cousin Elizabeth. We wanted to see her pregnant for ourselves. How thrilled we were for her and Zacharias. As well, I was eager to share my own amazing news.

But somehow Elizabeth already knew. For when we greeted each other, her unborn son jumped for joy inside her and she exclaimed: *"Oh Mary, blessed are you among women, and blessed is the fruit of your womb! But why is this granted to me, that the mother of my Lord should come to me? Blessed are you who believed, for there will be a fulfillment of those things which were told you by the messenger of the Lord."*

In joyous response, I sang again the words I first sang when Angel Gabriel came to me, the words inspired by Hannah's song of old: *"My soul magnifies the Lord, and my spirit has rejoiced in God my Savior."*

I stayed with Elizabeth to assist her until after her son John was born. What a glorious time we shared! I was still there when Zacharias was suddenly able to speak again. And I heard his prophetic hymn – the first announcement to the world that John would one day prepare the way of the Lord, my son. Back then in the midst of our joy, we couldn't have imagined that the future of our sons would also include martyrdom.

In fact, there was so much I didn't know and could never have guessed. Like moving to Bethlehem just before Jesus was born, and soon after fleeing to Egypt. Like the wonderful visits of the shepherds and wisemen who, by the way, came with their wives and families to welcome baby Jesus. Like the gifts from the wisemen that provided for our needs during our refugee years and long after in Nazareth. And like the wonderful years of Jesus' growing up with his brothers and sisters.

Ah yes, because of Jesus, our family life was divinely blessed. Looking back, I can see that for years he practiced telling parables and working miracles on us – and on other people and animals near him.

In woodworking skills, Jesus in time surpassed even Joseph. I remember the day he told his disciples that his *"yoke was easy."* I couldn't help smiling as I thought of the Galilean men who had waited months to purchase yokes carved by Jesus. They wanted only his yokes because his yokes made burden bearing so much easier for oxen as well as humans.

While life with Jesus was blessed, I'd be wrong to give the impression it was uneventful. Remember the time he stayed in Jerusalem at the Temple and frightened me so? Nor was that the last time I didn't know where he was for days or even weeks at a time.

But I learned not to worry and to commit him to God, his Father in heaven.

Like everyone else, I wasn't sure how Jesus' divine calling to deliver his people would be manifested. I kept waiting and watching and pondering. Then one day at a wedding reception in Cana, I felt something within compelling me to urge Jesus to reveal his heavenly purpose. If you aren't familiar with the story, review it in Saint John's Gospel. The wording is somewhat puzzling, but the outcome is clear. In spite of his reluctance, Jesus' divine ministry began publicly with that miraculous wedding punch event.

From then on, the few years left to Jesus passed so quickly.

As you might expect, I was one of his closest followers – and one of his first women disciples. Yes, Jesus had his circle of twelve men disciples. But as the Holy Gospels state, there were many others who were also his disciples, including numerous women.

Among Jesus' women disciples were my sister Salome and myself, the sisters Mary and Martha from Bethany, Mary Magdalene, the wife of Simon Peter whose name history has lost, Mary the mother of John Mark and her servant Rhoda, "Naomi" whose twelve-year hemorrhage Jesus healed, the "twins"

Joanna and Susanna, and my Aunt "Judith" who was the wife of Uncle Joseph of Arimathea.

When you read the Gospels carefully, you will note that many of us women were with Jesus just before his last Passover supper with his twelve disciples. And we were there right after the Last Supper, and all throughout the dreadful events that followed.

So where were we women disciples during the Last Supper?

Don't you suppose we were there with Jesus then too? Don't you suppose we prepared the Passover and served it as we had countless other meals?

Of course, we were there, as various ancient artworks in Europe of the Last Supper portray so magnificently. We just weren't there in Leonardo da Vinci's famous mural in Milan – the painting on the wall of a monastery dining hall (a good reason not to include women), the one that has dominated the perception of so many for so long, especially in America.

That unforgettable Passover night, I sensed Jesus would not become our Messiah in the way so many of us expected. He would not be a human King of the Jews. When he was put on trial for blasphemy and then so cruelly crucified, my soul was indeed pierced – ah, what agony, just as Simeon had prophesied.

But I never stopped trusting. I knew God would somehow keep His promise to me and to all the world. And He did – through my beloved son, His Holy Son, our resurrected Lord and Savior.

* * *

Indeed, I, Mary, the blessed mother of our Lord and one of his woman disciples, was an ordinary person transformed by the power of Jesus Christ.

You, too, can experience this transformation, and live or die for the glory of God.

Amen.

Meditation Passages:
Luke 1, 2; Matthew 2:13-18; 13:15,16; Mark 6:3;
John 2:1-12; 19:25-27; Acts 1:14.

Chapter 2

Salome: A Privileged Aunt Memoir of a Woman Disciple

I am Salome – the sister of Jesus' mother Mary, and one of Jesus' close followers present at the Last Supper. Since Jesus was my nephew, I was indeed a privileged aunt.

As you may recall from Biblical and historical records, before my marriage I was from Nazareth, located in the southern part of the province of Galilee. In Aramaic, Nazareth means "watchtower," a fitting name for my hometown that overlooked an important highway, and was frequented by trade caravans and Roman troops. Because traders and soldiers often camped in our community during their travels, other Jews liked to joke, "Can anything good come out of Nazareth?"

My nephew Jesus certainly changed that perception, didn't he?

In many ways, Nazareth was a good place to live in my time. Because of its usefulness to soldiers and traders, those of us who lived there were comparatively safe and prosperous. Many Nazarenes were skilled artisans and craftsmen – like my brother-in-law Joseph, a highly regarded woodcarver and carpenter. I'm not sure why my sister Mary and others of us from Nazareth have often been stereotyped as peasants, for in truth, we were not. Thanks to our location, we were some of the most cosmopolitan people in the Land of Palestine.

Many families living in the Nazareth area were from the Tribe of Judah, and like my family were descendants of the royal line of David. Had my sister Mary and I lived before the terrible wars and captivities of the Jewish people, we would be remembered today as Princess Mary and Princess Salome.

Ponder that a moment – makes calling my nephew *Prince of Peace* more meaningful, doesn't it?

Because of our royal heritage, my sister Mary and I were fortunate to have more privileges than many young women of our time. Although our own family's circumstances were reduced by misfortune, we had many caring, generous relatives. Among these was Uncle Joseph, who was the wealthy merchant from Arimathea. And I'm sure you remember hearing about our mother's cousin Elizabeth and her influential husband, Priest Zacharias.

As Mary and I were growing up, these relatives and others encouraged us to have strong faith in Yahweh. They urged us to study the Law with diligence. To them and our beloved mother Anne, we were not just girls, but girls with a special heritage and purpose. Who knew what Yahweh might require of us? We might become another Miriam or Deborah, Esther or Ruth, or even the mother of the promised Messiah. What Jewish young woman of my time didn't long for that wonderful possibility!

When my sister and I were old enough to marry, our mother and other relatives began the search for suitable husbands for us. Because Mother wanted us to have happy marriages, the search was not a hurried one. In time, I married Zebedee, a prosperous fisherman from Lake Galilee, and Mary married Joseph, a well-known carpenter from our hometown Nazareth.

Not only were Mary and I sisters, close in age, but we were each other's best friend. Even after our betrothals and marriages, we spent as much time together as we could. The distance between Capernaum where I lived and Nazareth only made our times together more precious.

When Mary told Mother and me about her visit from the angel Gabriel, my mother and I never doubted her miraculous conception. Nor did we permit our relatives and friends to say anything negative about her and Joseph in our presence. Fortunately, the prophetic message by Priest Zacharias, our cousin Elizabeth's husband, quickly helped to squelch gossip and rumors.

During the years Mary and Joseph and young Jesus were away in Bethlehem and then Egypt, Mary and I missed each other so much. It's probably hard for you in this day and age to imagine, but we had no contact at all with each other during those years. So you can understand how excited I was when they showed up dusty and weary at our door one hot summer evening. Because we had so much catching up to do, they stayed with us for several months before settling again in Nazareth.

That summer was the beginning of special bonding between my young son John and his cousin Jesus. The two were nearly the same age, and my son James was a doting older brother and cousin. The three often played together or did simple chores.

Even back then when they were so young, I could see my sons were taking after their father Zebedee, and were well on their way to becoming *the sons of thunder*. Jesus, as young as he was, amazed his mother and me more than once when he calmed his cousins with a look or a few childish words.

In those days, we didn't know what the future held. But we did know Jesus was somehow special, and that whatever became of him would affect us all. If he really became the King of the Jews, as we increasingly hoped he would, I looked forward to my sons being right there beside him, serving as his closest advisers. I even mentioned to Mary a couple of times how I liked to imagine the three of them grown up and dressed in royal robes, ruling over a peaceful and prosperous kingdom together.

She would look off into the distance as she replied, "Well, you know, Salome, God's ways are often not our ways. But I hope whatever happens, our families will always be there for each other."

And we were.

So naturally, I helped Mary prepare and serve the last Passover supper for Jesus and his band of twelve at the Jerusalem villa of our elderly Uncle Joseph from Arimathea. Joining us were Martha and her sister Mary from Bethany, Simon Peter's wife whose name history has forgotten, Mary the mother of John Mark and her servant Rhoda, "Naomi" whose twelve-year hemorrhage Jesus healed, the "twins" Joanna and Susanna, my dear friend Mary from Magdala, and of course, Aunt "Judith" in whose upper family room we gathered together that last evening.

Does finding that out about us women disciples surprise you?

It shouldn't.

When you read the Gospels carefully, you will note that many of us women were there with Jesus just before his last supper with his twelve closest disciples. And we were there right after the Last Supper, and all throughout the dreadful events that followed.

So don't you suppose we were right there with Jesus and the others during the Last Supper too? Don't you suppose we prepared the Passover and served it as we had countless other meals?

Yes, we were there, as various ancient artworks in Europe of the Last Supper portray. For a very good reason, we just weren't there in Leonardo da Vinci's celebrated painting on the monastery dining room wall in Milan.

But there was a time we were there for the Master no one dares question. It's too well documented, both in Biblical and historical accounts. We were there when Jesus was tried, and during the ordeal of his crucifixion and burial. Our sorrow was immense, but even then my awesome nephew Jesus reached out to us women in spite of his own unspeakable anguish.

As he dragged his cross in excruciating pain through the streets on his way to Golgotha, he gasped to us: *"Daughters of Jerusalem, do not weep for me, but weep for yourselves and for your children."*

How could we leave Jesus to suffer alone? He always thought of others before himself. Even though many of his other disciples fled in fear and shame, we could not.

How grateful we were when Uncle Joseph and Nicodemus secretly arranged with Pilate to bury Jesus. My son John, Jesus' beloved cousin and disciple, also helped. He had bravely stayed with my sister Mary and me throughout that entire ordeal, an arm supporting each of us.

You remember, don't you, Jesus' last words to his mother Mary from the cross? *"Woman, behold your son!"* Then to his cousin John, *"Behold your mother!"* From that moment on, my sister Mary made her home with us.

Standing in view of the cross on that terrible first Good Friday, how devastated we women were. But how quickly on the first Easter morning our weeping changed to joy when we discovered Jesus was alive again.

"He is risen! He is risen!" we shouted as we hurried to tell the other disciples.

Just several weeks later, we again exclaimed to each other and to anyone else listening. "He's ascended back into heaven! We saw Jesus rise up into the sky with our own eyes! He's returned to his Father in heaven to prepare a place for us!"

Yes, Mary was right all those years ago when she quietly and repeatedly reminded me that God's ways are often not our ways. I learned that regardless of what happens, being a follower of Christ is the best way to live – even when doing so leads to persecution, loss of wealth, or death. There is no way to adequately describe God's amazing grace through Jesus Christ. It can only be experienced.

No, I will never regret that my family and I followed Christ, and that we provided from our abundance for his ministry here on earth.

* * *

Indeed, I, Salome, privileged to be the aunt of our Lord and Master, was an ordinary person transformed by the power of Jesus Christ – as were my sons James and John, along many others in our family.

You, too, can experience this transformation, and live or die for the glory of God.

Amen.

Meditation Passages:
Matthew 20:20-28; Mark 15:40,41; 16:1;
Luke 23:44-49; John 19:25-27.

Chapter 3

"Naomi":
An Outcast No Longer
Memoir of a Woman Disciple

I am "Naomi" – and like my namesake in the Old Testament, Yahweh turned my bitter lot in life to joy. From the moment of Jesus' amazing miracle in my life, no longer was I an outcast. In gratitude, I became one of his close followers and providers. How then, I ask, could anyone doubt my presence at the Last Supper?

But first, perhaps you'd like to know who I am and why I once was an outcast.

Gladly will I tell you my story. For my greatest joy, as the meaning of my name suggests, is sharing how I was instantly healed by Jesus – especially when my testimony brings faith and hope to others who suffer or doubt.

My name "Naomi" is not given in the Bible with the story of my healing. But it is a fitting name for me because of what I suffered, as you will hear.

After I married, my home was beside Lake Galilee in the city of Capernaum – the city you no doubt recognize as the center of Jesus' ministry following his rejection by his hometown of Nazareth. On the day Jesus healed me, he was near Capernaum, ministering to the multitudes beside the lake. Thousands of people thronged around him, more people than I had ever before seen in one place. Because of my physical infirmity, I had been following Jesus since the previous day, hoping for a chance to be healed.

Ah yes, for many years I had sought healing. My life of bitterness began after my last child was born and my issue of blood did not cease. Not severe enough to end my life, my hemorrhage became my shame. For I was ceremonially unclean as long as I hemorrhaged. Mine was a family that carefully observed the Law, so I was isolated – an outcast in my own home, kept apart from my loved ones.

That's right! My husband and my older children were not permitted to touch me lest they, too, become unclean. No longer could I help my mother-in-law around the home. And when my precious baby reached his first birthday, I was forced to give him to the care of a wet nurse servant. After that sorrow, if a night passed when I didn't weep myself to sleep, I don't recall it.

Though we had wealth enough for the finest physicians, doctors of my time did not know the surgical treatments your modern doctors know. And after years of painful and humiliating treatments, at last I ceased trying to find a cure. I had spent so much money on seeking cures, the neighbors said I used up all our savings. Well, I certainly used up plenty, for I spent the amount of my dowry. That's when I accepted my case was hopeless. No more treatments would I endure. Nor would I spend the money of my children's family, even though my husband generously insisted.

After that, I rarely left home. I lived alone in a back room, finding comfort in the view of our green gardens reaching down to the blue lake and to the desert hills beyond. My family and servants talked to me from the door, and took care of my needs with gentle compassion. But ah, I was so alone and shamed. Over and over I begged God to show me my sin, so I could repent and be healed. Often in my heart I felt God's touch, but in my body there was no proof.

I still remember the pain of one of my life's worst days – the day my husband took another wife. At least he was God-fearing and didn't abandon me or drive me from his home. And he never failed to treat our children with love and kindness. He continued to speak tenderly to me from my door. He even brought his second wife's newborns to show me. But his second wife never came to my door. She was afraid my curse might pass to her if she came too close. I was afraid for her as well.

Sadly, one by one, my friends quit coming to my door to see me. And why not? I was unclean, an outcast in my own home and neighborhood. Who wants to have that kind of friend? I had to content myself with brief messages sent from time to time through my husband and children.

Ah yes, thinking about my children – have you been wondering what effect my infirmity had on them?

To my great relief, they were loving, obedient children. Since I couldn't touch them with love and discipline, it seemed God's angels did so for me. One blessing during those dark years were the hours my children spent at my door. As they reclined on special cushions their grandmother made for them, they talked with me and learned their lessons.

They especially loved listening to my stories. Sometimes my husband's other children came to listen too, as I told stories from the Holy Scrolls and from my childhood days. I even made up stories. One of our favorites was how someday, Yahweh would restore me to health. It was a day my children faithfully prayed for – though less and less often as the years passed.

Then came the day of my great surprise – the day Salome, wife of the fisherman Zebedee, suddenly appeared at my door. For minutes, my dear friend from years ago and I gazed at each other and wept, longing to hug each other as we once did.

"Naomi," she said, when she could speak. "I have great news for you. The one called Jesus of Nazareth is here beside the sea, teaching and healing. Have you heard of this man?"

"Yes," I answered. "Even in my isolation, I have heard many wonderful things about him. Are the stories really true, Salome? Is it true the son of your sister Mary is an amazing healer?"

"Yes, Naomi, yes!" Salome said with joy. "My sons James and John have joined his chosen band of twelve, so I know the truth with my own ears and eyes. That is why I have come. You must go to Jesus. He will heal you, Naomi. He will heal you. I am sure of it."

The rest of the day I paced my room, scarcely able to eat the food the servants brought. Not for a long time had I been so agitated. By nightfall, I had reached my decision. I would seek Jesus. I would seek Salome's nephew, the one I remembered as a special youth, playing with his cousins James and John.

But now he was a man, causing a great stir among our people and religious leaders. Yes, I would go to him.

That night I slept fitfully. Before dawn, I slipped away in secret from the house. It wasn't difficult to find Jesus, but it was impossible to get near him. Then on the second day as I followed him, I had my chance.

The distinguished ruler of our synagogue was making his way to Jesus. As his servants and the other religious leaders with him forced the people closest to Jesus to move aside, Jairus approached. Those of us in the crowd watched with awe. I noticed how Jairus had aged since the last time I was permitted to worship in the synagogue years ago.

Almost too late I realized my opportunity. Why, now I could get near Jesus while everyone's attention was focused on Jairus. My heart told me if I could but touch Jesus' clothes, I would be healed. For his clothes touched him, and somehow he touched Yahweh. Surely, I thought, no one would notice if I crept up and reached out the tips of my fingers to his cloak.

If you've read my story in the Gospels, you know that's exactly what I did. And my healing was instant. Perhaps you remember as well that in the days to follow, hundreds more did as I. They also were instantly healed.

The moment I was healed, I felt clean and strong again, feelings I had long forgotten. Joy filled my whole being. I wanted to hug Jesus and everyone around him. I wanted to sing out, "I am whole. I am clean. I'm restored. No longer am I an outcast."

Naturally, I didn't expect Jesus to notice me. But he did. And because he noticed, in a few minutes my fear and shame were gone forever. I could indeed sing aloud and dance in front of everyone. Ah yes, the joy of that day fills me still, and I'm sure there's no need for me to describe my welcome home that evening.

With arms around my beloved family, I repeated for them Jesus' wonderful words: *"Daughter, be of good cheer; your faith has made you well. Go home in peace."*

From then on, I was one of the women who followed the Master. I knew what I gave to Jesus' ministry from my husband's wealth could never repay God for our new life. But at least my family and I were saying, "Thank you, Lord. Thank you."

The other women disciples close to Jesus were much like me – we were all women who had been miraculously healed, or had witnessed our loved ones touched by him. Because of the gratitude and love in our hearts, we were constantly with him and his other close disciples. We were the ones who provided their meals, and arranged their accommodations in neighborhood homes. And we often ministered in special ways to the women and children in the multitudes around Jesus.

So don't you suppose we were right there during the Last Supper as well? Don't you suppose we prepared the Passover and served it as we had countless other meals?

Yes, we were there as various ancient artworks in Europe of the Last Supper portray. We just weren't there in Leonardo da Vinci's celebrated painting on the monastery dining room wall in Milan – the scene that has dominated the perception of so many, for so long, especially in America.

But there was a time we were there for the Master that no one dares question. It's too well documented, both in Biblical and historical accounts. We were there when Jesus was tried, and throughout the ordeal of his crucifixion and burial. Our sorrow was immense as we witnessed his unspeakable anguish. Because we did not leave him during his suffering as did many of his other disciples, we have often been called "the women of the cross."

Standing in view of the cross on that dreadful, first Good Friday, how devastated we women were.

But how quickly our weeping changed to joy on the glorious first Easter – the morning we discovered Jesus was truly alive again.

"He is risen! He is risen!" we shouted as we hurried to tell the others.

And I assure each of you pondering my words right now that Christ is indeed alive. And following him is life abundant, though doing so may lead to persecution, loss of wealth, or even death. I know what I'm saying, for all that happened to me.

The words Jesus said to Jairus and me one day so long ago, he still says: *"Don't be afraid; just believe."* Yes, Jesus' amazing grace will be with each of you through whatever valleys your walks of faith may lead. Of that, I am proof.

* * *

Indeed, I, "Naomi," whose life was changed from bitterness to abundant joy, was an ordinary person transformed by the power of Jesus Christ.

You, too, can experience this transformation, and live or die for the glory of God.

Amen.

Meditation Passages:
Matthew 9:18-26; Mark 5:21-43; Luke 8:40-56.

Chapter 4

Mary the Magdalene: An Early Church Leader Memoir of a Woman Disciple

I am Mary of Magdala – one of history's most controversial women, and one of Jesus Christ's women disciples present at the Last Supper.

I urge you to be careful what you read and assume about me, for there are many religious scholars as well as others who seek to discredit both the Master and me. Unfortunately, their speculations overlook definite clues about me in the Gospels.

But fortunately, the most significant event of my life is clearly recorded in the Bible and cannot be misunderstood – I was the first witness of our resurrected Lord. Isn't that amazing affirmation for women of all time, everywhere?

Because I was the first to speak with Jesus after his resurrection and then to tell the good news to his disciples, I was known in the early years of the Church as "an apostle to the apostles." Some even called me the "thirteenth apostle." That was before much of my life's story became hidden and then forgotten.

Indeed, my life was much like that of the twelve apostles, as the men disciples closest to Jesus came to be called. Like them, for many years I traveled widely to share the good news of the Messiah. I, too, started churches and performed many miracles in the name of our Lord. And like the twelve apostles, I instructed and encouraged the early believers. I even wrote a Gospel, though only fragments of it remain for today's scholars to debate.

With the passing of centuries, for some reason the record of my role in the early days of Christianity has faded and nearly disappeared in the Western church. But not in the Eastern churches. They still acknowledge the ancient traditions and celebrate how the Lord blessed and used my leadership.

Today there is a movement in the Catholic Church to return to the truth about me. For this I am grateful. I pray the movement will reach throughout Christendom wherever there is confusion and misinformation about me. And of course, I am grateful for the numerous institutions in existence today named for me. Why? Certainly not because of anything in me, but because they point to God's redeeming and healing power through Jesus Christ and the Holy Spirit.

Yes, I was a Magdalene, from that thriving port of Magdala on Lake Galilee. And yes, my hometown had harlots, as did many other places frequented by male travelers. But I assure you, most Jewish Magdalene women were honorable and sought to follow the Law.

So why do many today assume my life before the Master healed me was dishonorable? And why do some make unworthy inferences about Jesus and me?

I also wonder why I have been confused with another woman who followed Jesus – the one formerly an adulteress and the sister of Martha and Lazarus of Bethany. The Gospel writers tried to keep me identified by calling me a Magdalene, but still confusion has occurred. (By the way, here's a name tip if you need it: think of Magdalene as a name like Nazarene or American, not as my surname.)

Back to my story – in truth, I was considerably older than Jesus, near the age of his mother Mary and her sister Salome. Because my name was often listed first, some Bible scholars suggest I was the oldest and most influential of Jesus' women disciples.

Jesus' Aunt Salome and I became friends soon after she married Zebedee and moved to Capernaum near my home by the lake. Through Salome, I became a friend of her sister Mary who visited frequently. So I knew Jesus and his brothers and sisters from the time they were children playing with their cousins James and John and the others. And do you know something? Early on I sensed Jesus was special. For even when he was young, his presence soothed me and helped my dreadful physical condition.

Though I was a woman of independent means and with aristocratic status, for many years I suffered from a physical problem not even the best physicians could cure. I lived a life of privilege, yes, but my life was not normal, nor happy. For from time to time, demons seized me, tormented my body and threw me writhing and moaning to the ground.

These disruptions affected me not only physically and socially, but spiritually as well. I pled with Yahweh to show me my sin so I could repent and be healed. He did reveal my sin to me. But I was weak. I could not give up my secret idol fascination and worship. And so again and again, the demons of my hidden ivory goddess took control of me.

During my times free of seizures, I lived a scholar's life. What else could I do? I certainly couldn't marry and have a family. So I studied religion, language, philosophy, history and more.

Some of our family friends thought that was why demons came upon me, but we scoffed at that. In my family, females had long been given the advantages of learning, especially those of us blessed with good minds.

In fact, did you know that my scholarly interests are the reason Oxford and Cambridge Universities have colleges named after me? Ironic, isn't it, that for centuries after their founding, those colleges were for males only.

So you can see, when my time came to be a leader among Jesus' followers and in the early Church, I was ready. I eagerly used my abilities and inheritance for the Master. I was thrilled, as the Scriptures say, to be one of "*certain women who provided for Him from their substance.*" It was one way I could show my gratitude to the Lord for casting away my demons, and for revealing Yahweh, God of truth and light, to me. Furthermore, I wanted to make it possible for others, especially women, to find the spiritual joy and peace Jesus freely offers to those who follow him.

Following Jesus in person – those were the most wonderful three years of my life. And for the rest of my days, I never tired of telling the stories of Jesus to whoever would listen, especially to women and children.

I loved to tell about the Master's miracles – and there were far, far more than the few recorded in the Gospels.

I told about the time Jesus miraculously fed thousands and thousands of people by multiplying just a few fishburgers.

About the wedding reception, when in the blink of an eye, he turned ordinary water into the best-tasting punch imaginable.

And how during a fierce storm, he walked on top of the raging lake waters.

But best of all, I told how he healed untold numbers of people who suffered from permanent, incurable diseases and demons – just like he healed me, praise be to God.

In addition to Jesus' miracles, I deeply appreciated his intellectual side, especially when he stumped and embarrassed the proud religious rulers. And like Mary of Bethany, I spent time whenever I could sitting at Jesus' feet with his inner circle of disciples. What a joy to learn from him by listening and discussing. However, unlike Mary, I was not just contemplative. I also needed to be active like her efficient sister Martha. In fact, Martha and I often provided the meals for Jesus and his followers. Sometimes we served a dozen, sometimes hundreds.

So it shouldn't surprise you that Martha, her sister Mary and I were among the women who prepared and served the last Passover supper for the Lord. Joining us were Jesus' mother Mary and her sister Salome, the wife of Simon Peter whose name history has forgotten, Mary the mother of John Mark and her servant Rhoda, "Naomi" whose twelve-year hemorrhage Jesus healed, the "twins" Joanna and Susanna, and "Judith" the wife of Joseph of Arimathea in whose upper family room we gathered.

When you read the Gospels carefully, you will note that many of us women were with Jesus just before his last supper with his twelve closest disciples. And we were there right after the Last Supper, and all throughout the dreadful events that followed.

So where were we women during the Last Supper?

We were there with Jesus, as various ancient artworks in Europe of the Last Supper portray. For good reason, we just weren't there in Leonardo da Vinci's famous painting – the mural on the wall of the monastery dining hall in Milan.

But there was a time when we were there for the Master that no one can take away. It was too well documented, both in Biblical and historical accounts. We were there when Jesus was tried, and during his crucifixion and burial. Our sorrow was unspeakable, but even then Jesus reached out to us women in spite of his agony.

As he dragged his cross through the streets on his way to Golgotha, he gasped, *"Daughters of Jerusalem, do not weep for me, but weep for yourselves and for your children."*

How could we possibly leave Jesus to suffer alone? He always thought of others before himself. And even though many of his other disciples ran away in fear and shame, we women could not.

We were grateful when Joseph of Arimathea and Nicodemus were brave enough to bury Jesus. Jesus' beloved disciple and cousin John was also there helping. He had boldly stayed with his mother Salome and his Aunt Mary, Jesus' mother.

You remember, don't you, Jesus' words to his mother from the cross? *"Woman, behold your son!"* And then to his cousin John, *"Behold your mother!"*

And surely you remember the Master's words that glorious, wondrous morning when he appeared to me outside the empty tomb, alive.

"Woman," he said, *"why are you weeping? Whom are you seeking? Go now to my disciples and tell them I am ascending to my God and your God."*

Did anyone ever get to make a more triumphant announcement than I – the one I shouted out on that first Easter morning?

"He is alive! He is alive! The Master is alive!" I jubilantly shouted to his grieving and fearful disciples.

* * *

Indeed, I, Mary of Magdala and a woman disciple of the Master, was an ordinary person transformed by the power of Jesus Christ.

You, too, can experience this transformation, and live or die for the glory of God.

Amen.

Meditation Passages:
Luke 8:1-3; John 20:1-18; Acts 1:14.

Chapter 5

"Judith": Wife of Joseph of Arimathea Memoir of a Woman Disciple

I am "Judith" of Arimathea – the wife of Joseph the merchant who was a Jewish leader. And I am one of Jesus Christ's close followers present at the Last Supper.

Scarcely any records remain to tell my story, just a brief comment on my wifely status in the scrolls of the ancient historian Josephus. For as you know, in former days what women achieved was rarely recorded. That's one reason many of us excitedly followed Jesus – he cared about the experiences of women.

But the most important reason we followed him was because he reached our hearts with true spiritual love. We could sense his closeness to Yahweh, and his wisdom about life.

I ask you now to use your imagination as you focus on the possibilities of my life.

Do you remember reading in the Gospels about my beloved husband Joseph? He was a wealthy and powerful Jewish merchant, giving me more influence than most women enjoyed. Because of Joseph's position with the Jewish ruling council of the Sanhedrin, one of our homes was in Jerusalem. We had other lovely villas, as well as our home in Arimathea located midway between Jerusalem and the Mediterranean Sea.

Our wealth came from the shipping business Joseph inherited from his father. And it was our fleet of ships that eventually saved our lives. But more about that later.

During the calm months of the year, Joseph and I often journeyed aboard one of our merchant ships to different Mediterranean ports. One summer, that's what we were doing when a freak, violent storm arose. I was terrified! I had never seen the sea so turbulent! I feared at any moment our ship might sink.

On that journey, we happened to have along several young relatives to keep our own children company. One of these was Joseph's great-nephew, the teenager Jesus of Nazareth. In those days, we didn't fully realize who he was, nor the extent of his powers. To our amazement, he didn't get seasick or frightened when the fierce storm threatened our lives and drove our ship off course.

In fact, he came to us and suggested with gentle authority, "Uncle Joseph and Aunt Judith, we've been blown close to a strange land. A sheltered cove lies a short ways to the north where we can drop anchor until the storm passes. Command the sailors to cease struggling against the gales, and let the ship be taken to where we will not be harmed."

Back then we didn't know the name of the place, but in a few minutes we had miraculously reached the coast of what you now call England, near Glastonbury. Years later, we remembered the cove when we had to flee for our lives. So that idyllic spot became not just a temporary refuge for us, but also our last home on earth. Interestingly, living there eventually connected us to the marvelous King Arthur tradition of Great Britain.

How could we have known then that the chalice we brought with us because the Master used it during his last Passover supper would become the Holy Grail? Or that this Holy Grail would be an inspiration to millions of Christians throughout the centuries?

Ah yes, the Lord's Last Supper. It's time to focus on that holy evening.

When Christians recite the "Apostle's Creed," one of the lines is this: "*I believe in the communion of Saints.*" Have you pondered the meaning of those words?

Those words mean that the spirits of us Christians who have already departed this earth actually commune or visit with those of you still alive. God mysteriously uses us to encourage you in the faith. However, many people of faith these days are no longer sensitive to this kind of mystical experience. And I must say, I have to laugh sometimes when I'm here to commune with you and I see your representations of the Lord's Last Supper. Too often these portrayals show only Jesus and his twelve closest men disciples.

Fortunately, various ancient artworks are more accurate. They portray others of us who were there for that special Passover meal – which, by the way, was a Jewish family Seder celebration.

How do I know who was there? Why, that celebration took place away from the dirt and noise of the city in the upper room of our Jerusalem home – or as you might express it, in our rooftop family room.

Because Joseph was a member of the Sanhedrin, at first we were secret followers of Christ, but certainly not inactive ones. Our spacious, comfortable homes were quietly open to the Master and those accompanying him whenever needed. The Last Supper was one of those occasions. We even sent a servant with a donkey to guide Jesus and his disciple to our hillside home after his triumphant entry into Jerusalem.

Throughout that memorable day, other women who were disciples of Jesus helped me prepare the Passover potluck. Mary, Jesus' mother and my husband Joseph's niece, had come with her sister Salome the day before to help. As did Martha and her sister Mary from nearby Bethany. Passover morning, others came. Mary Magdalene, Simon Peter's wife, Mary the mother of John Mark and her servant Rhoda, "Naomi" whose twelve-year hemorrhage Jesus healed, and the "twins" Joanna and Susanna – they all came to share in preparing and partaking of the Passover meal.

That evening, many members of our families also joined us in the special meal with Jesus and his disciples. After my husband led the Passover ritual, Jesus and his band of twelve closest disciples ate in the places of honor. The rest of us served and ate wherever we could find a spot to sit or stand. Many of the younger ones ate outside in the grove of olive trees where Jesus and others later went to pray.

But the joy of the evening didn't last long. For months we had feared something terrible might happen to Jesus. Threats to his life had been increasing – including from the Sanhedrin, to my husband's great chagrin. And alas, that night after the Passover meal, Jesus was arrested.

For some time, ships from our fleet had waited for us in Joppa in case we needed to flee quickly. And sure enough, after Jesus was executed and buried in our family tomb, our lives were threatened. Our connections to the Master were secret no longer. Nor did we want them to be. By the time Jesus arose from the dead and ascended to heaven, praise be to God, we were ready to forsake all and become public witnesses for our Lord and Savior.

The historian Josephus recorded that our family lost all our wealth and property when we fled from Jerusalem, as well as family members. That's not completely true, for we did save some of our possessions and several ships from our fleet.

However, we did lose several family members. But that was their brave choice. And they died victoriously. They boldly chose to remain in the Jerusalem area and be counted as Christ's followers. We were told they cried out to the very end of their torturous deaths, "Remember the Lord!" Yes, like so many others, they experienced God's amazing grace in their hour of greatest need.

When Joseph and I reached Joppa, we filled our ship with those willing to join us and with what valuables we had managed to bring along. We fled across the Mediterranean to the English cove we had discovered so long ago. We sensed the Spirit of the Lord miraculously directing us there again, just as had happened many years before.

Some may say it cost us too much to follow the Master. But we say, look how God provided a new home for us, and led us to people eager to hear about Christ and follow his true ways.

Should you travel today to Glastonbury, you can still visit places dear to us and hear the stories of miracles that happened. But the Holy Grail – is it there? Ah, dear friends, I know where it is, but I can't tell you. For God doesn't want you to follow the Grail, but rather the way of the risen Christ it mysteriously represents.

* * *

Indeed, I, "Judith," wife of Joseph of Arimathea and a woman disciple of the Master, was an ordinary person transformed by the power of Jesus Christ.

You, too, can experience this transformation, and live or die for the glory of God.

Amen.

Meditation Passages:
Matthew 27:57-61; Mark 15:42-47;
Luke 23:50-56; John 19:38-42.

Chapter 6

An Unnamed Woman: the Wife of Simon Peter Memoir of a Woman Disciple

I am an unnamed woman from Capernaum – the wife of Simon Peter, and one of Jesus Christ's women disciples present at the Last Supper.

Unnamed as I am in Biblical and historical records, be assured my name is written in the *Lamb's Book of Life*. For I was a close follower of God's Lamb, the Messiah of the world. And that's all that really matters, isn't it!

Though I am not named in the Gospels, nor even by the Apostle Paul when he mentioned to the Corinthians my travels with my husband Peter, the most important events of my life were recorded – of which the most important was living for the Master. But dying for his sake came next.

Perhaps you already know I was crucified along with Peter in Rome in 61 A.D. Side by side, we had served the Master throughout our lives. And for his sake, side by side we were martyred.

Thinking they could break Peter by making him witness my crucifixion, I was nailed on my cross first. But those ungodly, brutal Roman soldiers didn't know Peter. He was a true "rock" for the Master's Church. And they didn't know me. Above all, they didn't know the powerful grace of our Lord that sustains his followers in their times of greatest need.

On our crosses, Peter, who was upside down, gasped to me again and again, *"Remember the Lord!"* And I cried back to him those words of the martyrs. As we remembered the Lord's sacrifice for us, we were filled with grace to die for our Savior's sake. In spite of our agony, we did not deny Christ, nor did we betray our Christian sisters and brothers.

Now let me share with you more of our story.

Because we followed the Master, Peter and I lived extraordinary lives. Some would say the circumstances of our lives were fearsome. I agree. Some would say adventuresome. I agree. Some would say unbelievable. Again I agree. And some would say our lives were blessed. The last analysis is the best.

My blessed life of following the Master alongside my husband Peter actually started with the dynamic preaching of John the Baptist. Like most

Jews, Peter and I longed to be free from the oppressive rule of the Romans. Yes, we were financially well-off, thanks to my father-in-law Jonah's prosperous fishing partnership with Zebedee. But still we chaffed at the cruel demands of the Roman government – especially at their idolatrous religious practices.

How we longed for the coming of the Messiah promised for centuries by Yahweh, and for the peaceful kingdom the Messiah would establish for us, God's chosen people.

My husband Peter was a huge man, so tall and muscular that everyone called him "the big fisherman." As he strode along the docks and through streets with his hand on his sword, no one dared challenge him, not even Roman soldiers. I always felt safe with him. And as you might expect, he made a great bodyguard for Jesus.

For years, the Zealots and Assassin Iscariots tried to get Peter to join them in their secret plotting to overthrow Rome. But thankfully, his brother Andrew always helped me talk him out of it. We reminded Peter of their father Jonah's words: "Wait, my sons, wait for the Messiah, our promised Prince of Peace. Men who live by the sword will die by the sword. We Jews have suffered enough from wars and executions. Let us wait for the Messiah."

I don't know how much longer Peter would have waited. He was an impatient and impetuous man, used to getting his own way. But fortunately, John the Baptist came along. I actually heard John before Peter did. Some of my friends heard him, then told me about him with great excitement. Several days later, I left my mother in charge of the children and the servants for a day, and went to hear John for myself.

The message of this godly, wilderness man gripped my heart and changed my life.

That night as we supped, all I could talk about was John the Baptist and his message. For once, Peter kept silent and listened. The next day, he and Andrew left the fleet in charge of our fishing company's chief steward and went to hear John for themselves.

Well, you know how one thing leads to another. Before long, John was imprisoned, then beheaded. But not before he introduced us and hundreds of others to his cousin Jesus – the amazing young teacher and healer from Nazareth who was causing such a stir among the Jews.

"Truly, this man must be the Messiah," we heard folks saying wherever we went. After he healed my mother, we were also convinced.

I remember well the day the Master asked the disciples who they thought he really was. As usual, my husband Peter blurted out an answer first, *"You are the Messiah, the Son of the living God!"*

In awe, the rest of us there that day agreed and said, "Yes, Lord, yes, you are the Messiah!"

I expected something grand and dramatic to happen at that moment. Like Jesus suddenly becoming a crowned king before our eyes, with vast armies appearing around him. That's what my heart expected. I think others felt the same way, because I saw them looking around.

But nothing changed, at least not visibly.

Peter and I lived by a large body of water called Lake Galilee. It always seemed to me that people who live around water are different from other people. Don't you agree?

The lakeside people I knew were strong and hard working. We formed close, loyal bonds with each other. We were more open and daring than confined city people. We enjoyed spectacular sunrises and sunsets over the water, and expected our lives to have inspiring moments like that to balance the grief of tragedies. We trusted easily in God's power because we experienced it every day. We believed in Satan too, because we also knew the power of evil.

But more than anything, as people we wanted to be free – free like the water that surrounded us. And that's what made the Roman occupation so bitter to bear. That's why we eagerly reached out for the spiritual truth and freedom offered by the Master. With our hearts free and redeemed, what did our bodies matter? John the Baptist first taught us that, and prepared us to follow Jesus.

After John's martyrdom, those of us who were Jesus' closest followers became increasingly concerned for his safety, as well as for our own. Threats of stoning reached us, so for a while we stayed away from Jerusalem, often moving about in secret.

We tried to persuade Jesus not to go to Bethany when word came of Lazarus' illness and death just before the Passover. But Jesus would not be deterred, so Thomas persuaded the rest of us to go along,

"Let us also go, that we may die with him if need be," Thomas kept repeating.

I thought to myself that if Thomas and my husband Peter were going to die for the Master, then so would I.

When you read the Gospels carefully, you will note that many of us women were in Bethany when Jesus raised Lazarus from the dead just before that last Passover meal. And we were there right after the Last Supper, and all throughout the dreadful events that followed.

So where were we women during the Last Supper?

Don't you suppose we were there with Jesus then too? Don't you suppose we prepared the Passover and served it as we had countless other meals?

Of course, we were there, as various ancient artworks of the Last Supper portray. For good reason, we just weren't there in Leonardo da Vinci's famous painting on the wall of the monastery dining hall in Milan – the mural that has dominated the perception of so many for so long.

So don't be surprised when I tell you that in addition to myself being present at the Last Supper, there were other women, too – Mary of Magdala, Martha and her sister Mary of Bethany, "Naomi" whose twelve-year hemorrhage Jesus healed, the "twins" Joanna and Susanna, "Judith" the wife of Joseph of Arimathea, Mary the mother of John Mark and her servant Rhoda, Salome, and of course her sister Mary who was Jesus' beloved mother.

During Jesus' dreadful ordeal that Passover weekend, our sorrow was unspeakable. But in spite of his agony, Jesus reached out to us women as he dragged his cross through the streets on his way to Golgotha.

"Daughters of Jerusalem," he groaned, *"do not weep for me, but weep for yourselves and for your children. For if this is what is done to the innocent, then what will be done to the guilty?"*

How could we leave Jesus to suffer alone? He always thought of others before himself. And even though many of his other disciples ran away in fear and shame, including my husband Peter, we women could not. Later, I would help Peter deal with his denial of the Master. But that night, I knew my place was as near to my suffering Lord as possible, regardless of where my husband fled.

I don't think I need to tell you any more of my story. Surely you already know the next wonderful events. How Jesus came forth from the tomb, gloriously alive again! How during his last few days on earth, he ministered to us, his followers. How he spoke those special words of forgiveness to Peter, "*Feed my lambs.*" Then how he ascended into heaven.

What an awesome sight that was – a sight that inspired Peter and me to keep traveling and sharing the Gospel of our Lord for the rest of our lives, even during our cruel deaths on crosses side by side.

* * *

Indeed, I, the unnamed wife of Simon Peter and a woman disciple of the Master, was an ordinary person transformed by the power of Jesus Christ.

You, too, can experience this transformation, and live or die for the glory of God.

Amen!

Meditation Passages:
Matthew 8:14-17; Mark 1:29-31;
Luke 4:38-41; I Corinthians 9:6.

Chapter 7

Martha: the Sister of Mary from Bethany Memoir of a Woman Disciple

I am Martha of Bethany – the sister of Mary and Lazarus, and one of Jesus Christ's close followers present at the Last Supper. When you think of the Gospel accounts of my meal serving, who more fitting than I to be there!

But before we think about that unforgettable Passover night, you need to know more of my background.

When you read carefully the passages from the Gospels that tell about Mary, Lazarus and me, you will find that Simon, a healed leper, was from our same home in Bethany. Of course, for he was my husband and the source of our wealth At least, that's what some Bible scholars think. I'd also like to suggest to you that he was one of the ten lepers Jesus healed in the Gospel accounts – the one that returned to say "thank you." From that time on, he and I and

Mary and Lazarus were all close followers of the Master.

Although it's interesting to ponder the details of our lives, probably none of them matters much any more. All that really matters is that we were a household who followed the Master, and often welcomed him and his disciples to our comfortable, spacious home.

Our hometown was a delightful place to live, especially if you were from a well-connected family like mine. Bethany was located on the gentle, eastern slope of the Mount of Olives, so our home was surrounded by beautiful olive orchards. Thanks to the climate and moisture, there were also many fig orchards. In fact, Bethany means "house of figs," and is a name long associated with beauty and fruitfulness.

Some Bible scholars suggest I was older than Mary and Lazarus. As such, I naturally assumed a position of leadership in our home. I loved to entertain and cook for our friends and important guests. But to be honest, we had plenty of servants, so mostly I just supervised. Nonetheless, I was known for my delicious, kosher dinners.

Do you want to know my most important cooking secret?

Fresh oil from the first-press of tree-ripened olives – only oil like that can produce the best flavors in vegetables and sauces. I could never understand why some of our neighbors sold their first-press oil. I always kept ours for cooking and for gifts. We sold the second- and third-presses instead.

Because the area of Bethany was so fertile, I rarely saw harsh poverty. And our close proximity to Jerusalem – only two miles – made us a bedroom community for many wealthy families from that great city. The presence of wealth accustomed those of us who lived there to luxuries.

So you can see, in spite of Roman oppression, I was a privileged woman. But since my family worshiped Yahweh, I still prayed daily that the Messiah would come soon to deliver my people from the Romans and re-establish the Kingdom of Israel.

And just think – the Messiah did come in my time. But his kingdom certainly wasn't what I had been taught to expect.

My brother Lazarus was the first of my family to see and hear Rabbi Jesus. He heard him teach in our synagogue one Sabbath. I don't recall why, but Mary and I were absent from the women's balcony that day.

The next day, I instructed servants to prepare a picnic lunch, and the three of us walked to the nearby countryside to hear the young rabbi healer from Nazareth. We had heard about the crowds following him, but that day multitudes of people were packed around him. To be heard, Rabbi Jesus went part way up the Mount of Olives to teach from a position that amplified his voice to the throngs listening in the valley.

I remember well the sermon he preached to us from the Mount.

Jesus spoke these words and more: "*Blessed are the poor in spirit, for theirs is the Kingdom of Heaven. Blessed are those who mourn, for they shall be comforted. Blessed are those who hunger and thirst for righteousness, for they shall be filled.*"

That was our condition, all right. Mary, Lazarus and I hungered to understand God's ways. We longed to feel the peace of salvation in our hearts. No wonder John the Baptist proclaimed Jesus to be the Messiah. That day, something within me agreed with John.

After we had listened to Jesus for several hours, I suggested to Lazarus, "Find out if Jesus and his disciples need a place to eat and sleep tonight. If they do, invite them to our home."

Lazarus questioned a disciple standing near us. The disciple named Simon Peter accepted our invitation thankfully and without surprise. He said the Master had told him earlier a place would be provided for them in Bethany that night.

Mary and I hurried home to supervise the preparations. We were so excited and said to each other, "Might this man be the promised Messiah? Praise be to God! Let us follow him and find out."

That night was the first of countless times that Jesus and his disciples stayed with us. Sometimes there were just twelve disciples. Sometimes there were many more. But we always managed to have enough food and sleeping pallets for the hungry, weary band.

When Jesus traveled to other places, we often went, too – usually with servants, provisions and tents. Not all villages had homes where Jesus could rest, and my family was glad to help out whenever we could.

There were other women and their families who helped as well. And like me, they were among those present at the Last Supper. The women I remember who helped prepare and serve the last Passover meal for Jesus were his mother Mary and her sister Salome, Mary of Magdala, "Naomi" whose twelve-year hemorrhage Jesus healed, the "twins" Joanna and Susanna, "Judith" the wife of Joseph of Arimathea, Mary the mother of John Mark and her servant Rhoda, and of course, my sister Mary.

My sister Mary was the one who anointed the Master with a fragrant lotion as he dined in our home one evening. Though they were our guests and friends, some of the disciples protested aloud because of her background and what they called her waste.

But Jesus defended her love offering with these words: *"Let her alone. She has done a good work for me. She has come beforehand to anoint my body for burial. Wherever the Gospel is preached in the whole world, what she has done will be told as a memorial to her."*

Doesn't that make you want to know what following Jesus did for my beloved sister Mary?

Whatever you may have heard, Mary was not a woman of the streets. But yes, she was an adulteress. She loved a man who would not marry her because his family objected. There were other men who wanted to marry her, for she was lovely in looks and person, and had a generous dowry. But Mary always said she would never marry a man she didn't love. A woman with money can say those words. So in that regard, she was fortunate. But in another regard, she was not. She only loved the one man, and so she never married.

Then Rabbi Jesus came into our lives.

Because of his teachings, Mary's life was transformed. Soon, all she cared about were spiritual matters. The sins in her life were forgiven and she sinned no more. Remember Anna, the elderly prophetess who lived in the Temple? That's what Mary became – a woman dedicated to God because of His Son, Jesus Christ, our marvelous friend.

At first, I didn't realize what had happened in Mary's heart. That's why I was irritated the evening she spent so much time with Jesus instead of helping me. Then Jesus' words opened my eyes to the new person she was becoming. Ah, how I rejoiced. My prayers were answered, and I had been too busy to notice.

I wonder, has that ever happened to you?

It's been said Mary, Lazarus, and I were some of Jesus' best friends. Indeed we were, and that's why Mary and I couldn't understand why Jesus didn't come immediately when we sent word to him that Lazarus had a fatal illness.

But you already know what happened, don't you!

What Jesus did for Lazarus was another amazing example of God bringing good from something that seemed so awful. And just think of the untold numbers who have believed in Christ because Lazarus was restored to life!

So you can understand that those of us who witnessed what happened to Lazarus were not about to leave Jesus' side. Oh yes, we had heard the death threats, and in our hearts we wondered if any of us were safe. But whether we were men or women, we went with him anyway to Jerusalem to commemorate the Passover.

When thousands of people cheered the Master's entry to Jerusalem, our hopes rose. Perhaps no one will dare harm him after all, we murmured to each other. But Jesus' popularity with the people only made matters worse for him with the Sanhedrin Council.

While the Gospel writers don't specifically say we women were at the Last Supper, they clearly note we were there right before and right after that Passover meal. So surely, we must have been there during the meal too – just as various ancient artworks of the Last Supper portray. We just weren't there in Leonardo da Vinci's famous mural -- the one painted on the wall of a monastery dining hall in Milan, and the most accepted portrayal of the Last Supper throughout Christendom.

Alas, only a few hours after the Last Supper, one dreadful event after another happened. And many of us women disciples witnessed everything. Jesus had changed our lives! We couldn't let him suffer such agony alone. During his terrible ordeal, the words I said to him a short while before in

Bethany kept coming back to me and giving me courage.

"Lord, I believe that you are the Christ, the Son of God," I had said. *"I believe you are the Messiah who is to come into the world. Lord, I believe. Lord, I believe."*

After I witnessed his miraculous resurrection and glorious ascension, I had enough courage to be a witnessing believer to the end of my life.

How about you? Do you believe in the Christ? Are you ready to follow him to the end of your life?

* * *

Indeed, I, Martha of Bethany and a woman disciple of the Master, was an ordinary person transformed by the power of Jesus Christ.

You, too, can experience this transformation, and live or die for the glory of God.

Amen!

Meditation Passages:
Mark 14:1-11; Luke 10:38-42;
John 11:1-48; 12:1-11.

Chapter 8

Joanna and Susanna: "Twin" Followers of Christ Memoir of Two Women Disciples

Joanna: Greetings in the name of our Lord, Jesus Christ. I am Joanna.

Susanna: And I am Susanna. We are "twin sisters" who were among Jesus' close women followers. Gladly did we follow Jesus, for he healed our infirmities and opened our hearts to his truth.

Joanna: Like some others who followed Jesus, I helped provide for our Lord and his group of closest followers. This I could do because I was the much-loved wife of a wealthy and generous Roman centurion.

Susanna: Yes, Joanna's husband Chuza was indeed generous, as well as kind. When my own husband Gaius was killed in a sword fight, my children and I were left in difficult circumstances, partly because of his gambling debts. My good brother-in-law was quick to suggest we live in his household. Since Joanna and I were often together in her home anyway, my children adjusted well to the change in our lives.

Though I regret to say so, I have to admit our lives improved after Gaius' unexpected death. He had been increasingly oppressed by dark thoughts, causing him to drink too much wine. Then he was unkind and cruel to others, even to his family – especially after he lost bets on gladiator and animal fights.

Joanna: Every word Susanna tells you is the sad truth. Oh, how we wish her husband had lived to meet Jesus like we did. I am sure Jesus could have brought light and joy to Gaius, and transformed him into a happier, kinder man.

Yes, the most amazing day of our lives was the day we met the impressive young teacher and healer from Nazareth. But before we share about that, perhaps we should first tell you how two Jewish sisters happened to marry Roman soldiers.

Susanna: Actually, in our time, Jewish girls marrying Romans was fairly common. Many Jews did not practice their religion faithfully, often ignoring the law against marrying Gentiles. Ironic, isn't it, since that was one of the reasons why

Yahweh allowed his chosen people to be conquered and scattered throughout the world – a lesson many of us Jews obviously never learned.

Joanna: No, our parents were certainly not orthodox Jews. Like their own parents, they paid only token attention to the cumbersome laws of our religion – except during times of trouble. Then they hurried to Jerusalem to present offerings at the Temple and cry out to Yahweh, "Why, God? Why us?"

Our ancestors lived in several foreign countries before settling in Capernaum, that bustling crossroads city located on the Sea of Tiberias, By the way, do you know the Sea of Tiberias is the Roman name for the Sea of Galilee and better known today as Lake Galilee? In our time, it was named to honor Emperor Tiberius, as was the capital city of the area.

Susanna: Getting back to our story – to survive, our family adapted to the cultures around us, even keeping secret that we were Jews when need be. That way, we didn't get into unnecessary trouble, and it was easier to prosper.

Joanna: The men and boys in our family were boat builders, the trade that brought our great-grandfather and his sons and their families to Capernaum. Back then, Capernaum was an important boat building center. The Jews needed boats for their fishing fleets. The Romans needed ships to transport legions of soldiers and to fight sea battles. And everyone needed boats, small and large, for transportation.

Because of Capernaum's importance in the Province of Galilee, people from many places lived there or passed through - Jews, Romans, Greeks, Ethiopians, Egyptians, and others. Intermarriage became common and accepted - especially as more and more people became Roman citizens.

Susanna: When we reached marriageable age, our parents asked us about our husband preferences. We could be somewhat choosy, they said, because we had large dowries and came from a prominent family.

Joanna and I were identical in so many ways all our lives, and our choices for husband were identical, too. During puberty, we often discussed marriage and babies, especially with our personal servants who knew much more about men than we did.

Joanna: So we had our answer ready, and told our parents we wanted to marry men with position and money. It didn't matter what country or city they came from, or whether they were religious or not. But we did want husbands who weren't too old, ones who would be generous and promise to treat us like partners instead of property.

"What about marrying Roman centurions?" Father asked us.

We giggled and said that would be fine. The centurions we knew lived in big villas and were important officials in the area. People on the streets bowed to them as they passed, and their women rode in ornate sedan chairs carried by servants or slaves.

Susanna: Not long after our sixteenth birthday, we had a double wedding in a lavish Roman style. During the time of the festivities, we felt like princesses. But as you heard earlier, my princess feeling didn't last. Soon I found out Gaius had two very different personalities. And every year that passed, his dark side grew darker and more dominant.

Joanna was far more fortunate in her marriage. In time, she and Chuza developed a deep love for each other. So it was actually a relief to move with my children into a home where love and caring prevailed, instead of anger and abuse.

Joanna: We first met Jesus the day after he healed my husband Chuza's servant. Do you remember the Gospels' account of that miracle? This is how the physician Luke told it:

Jesus entered Capernaum. And a certain centurion's servant, who was dear to him, was sick and ready to die. So when he heard about Jesus, he sent elders of the Jews to Him, pleading with Him to come and heal his servant. And when the elders came to Jesus, they begged Him earnestly, saying that the one for whom He should do this was deserving, for he loves Israel, and has built us a synagogue.

Then Jesus went with them. And when He was not far from the house, the centurion sent friends to Him, saying, "Lord, do not trouble Yourself, for I am not worthy that You should enter under my roof. I did not even think myself worthy to come to You. But say the word, and my servant will be healed."

When Jesus heard these words, He marveled at the centurion, and turned around and said to the crowd that followed Him, "I say to you, I have not found such great faith, not even in Israel!" And those who were sent, returned to the house and found the servant well who had been sick.

Naturally, having something so wondrous happen in our household made all of us want to see and hear Jesus. We wanted to thank him for healing my husband's servant who had been with Chuza since his childhood and was like a dear uncle.

The day after the healing, many from our household went with us to the lakeshore to hear Jesus. We took along great quantities of provisions so we would have enough to share with Jesus and his close followers. Remember, there weren't any McDonald's or Pizza Huts back then.

At the end of that memorable day, both Susanna and I joined the other women disciples of Jesus. Chuza gave us his blessing to follow Jesus, and told us he would gladly help provide for Jesus ministry. Chuza said his only regret was that he couldn't join Jesus as well. But of course, his position as chief steward in the palace of Herod Antipas prevented that.

You may find this hard to believe, but Chuza became interested in our Lord because of discussions he and Herod Antipas had about religion. The Herod that Chuza worked for was the son of the Herod who ordered the murder of all those babies in Bethlehem when Jesus was born. He was also the one who very reluctantly ordered the beheading of John the Baptist in return for his teenage stepdaughter's seductive dance.

Herod Antipas was convinced the Jewish religion was true. And he was afraid Jesus was John the Baptist sent back by God to punish him. Herod wanted to know everything about Jesus that Chuza knew.

What Herod didn't know was that his worried questions caused my husband to believe in Jesus and God. Just as Jesus marveled at Chuza's faith, so did all of us in his household. And because of Chuza, we believed in Jesus, too.

In the years that followed, Chuza brought the Good News of the Master to thousands of seekers before he was burned to death as one of Nero's torches in Rome. His last words to his loved ones were, "Fear not! Remember the Lord who is with us always!"

Susanna: After learning what you have of our story, it shouldn't surprise you that Joanna and I were among the women who prepared and served the last Passover supper for the Lord. We were there working together with Jesus' mother Mary and her sister Salome, Mary of Magdala, Martha and Mary of Bethany, Mary the mother of John Mark and her servant Rhoda, the wife of Simon Peter, "Naomi" whose twelve-year hemorrhage Jesus healed, and "Judith" the wife of Joseph of Arimathea in whose home the Last Supper took place.

We were also there during the anguishing ordeal of Jesus trial and crucifixion. Because of Chuza's position as chief steward to Herod, I was able to take the other women to wherever Jesus was taken that night.

And we were on hand soon after for that glorious morning of Jesus' resurrection – as well as later when he ascended to heaven!

* * *

Indeed, we, Joanna and Susanna, "twin sisters" and married to Roman centurions, were among Jesus' close women followers. We were ordinary women transformed by the power of Jesus Christ.

You, too can experience this transformation, and live or die for the glory of God.

Amen.

Meditation Passages:
Luke 8:1-3; 24:1-12.

Chapter 9

Mary: John Mark's Mother and Rhoda's Owner Memoir of a Woman Disciple

I am Mary – the mother of John Marcus, or Mark as we usually called him. And I am the woman in whose home Rhoda was a servant. We three were among Jesus' close followers. As such, we were present at the Last Supper.

Living as we did in Jerusalem, we were active in the early Christian church. What amazing blessings from Yahweh we experienced! Gladly will I reveal to you now a little of my story.

Like some of the other women who followed Jesus, I helped provide for our Lord and his band of close followers. This I rejoiced to do, for I was a Jewish woman of independent means. I was the widow of "Philip" of Alexandria who came from a family of prominent Greek merchants.

That's how it happened our son Marcus, named for his paternal grandfather, was both Jew and

Greek, not uncommon in Jerusalem during our time. So it was natural for Mark later in his life to move to Alexandria to establish the Christian church there and became its first bishop.

But back to my story.

I expect you know that my name Mary in Greek or Miriam in Hebrew has long been a popular name for Jewish girls. Since Jesus' time, it has also been popular among Christians, but to honor a different namesake, his mother – whereas Jewish Marys are named after Moses' esteemed sister Miriam. In fact, we were named in the hope one of us Marys would someday bring into the world the ultimate deliverer, the promised Messiah of the Jews.

And that's exactly what happened to one of my dearest friends, Mary of Nazareth.

Even though I bear a famous name, I'm better known for my son Mark and my servant girl Rhoda than for myself. Their voices have been remembered in the Bible and by tradition far clearer than mine. But I wonder, would they have followed the Master if I had not done so first? Frightening, isn't it, to ponder the eternal effect of some of life's quickest choices! Daily I praise God that when it came to following Jesus, I made the right choice.

Before my marriage to "Philip," my home was Cyprus – that island lush with green forests and surrounded by the sparkling Mediterranean Sea. There my brother Barnabas and I grew up in beauty and privilege. In the decades to come, we both agreed that no matter where we traveled for our Lord, no other place ever compared, not even the magnificent Holy City of Jerusalem where I lived for many years.

I moved to Jerusalem when I married. There my husband died suddenly in his sleep one night when Mark was a small boy. My brother Barnabas nobly endeavored to fill the void. He insisted young Mark and I spend the summers in Cyprus. And Barnabas visited us in Jerusalem several times a year, sometimes bringing along a cousin or two to play with Mark. In fact, it was during one of my brother's visits I first heard of the one called Jesus of Nazareth.

How well I still remember the day Barnabas urged me to check out a new miracle-working rabbi he had heard about on his voyage from Cyprus. Not wanting to be seen near Jesus, Barnabas was eager for me to go and see what I thought. Together we discussed this remarkable and controversial man long into the night. We wondered: could a carpenter from Galilee be the Messiah we Jews had long awaited, especially questioning Jews like us?

Mark was a teenager at the time, and asked to go with me in my search for Jesus. My son was an extraordinary youth, with no cynicism or bitterness in his heart, but instead a great longing to know the truth. So you may wonder why I was reluctant to tell him "yes." I was reluctant because I feared he might become fascinated by another desert weirdo like John the Baptist.

The year before, we had gone to the Jordan River to hear the son of Priest Zacharias. Mark's keen interest in that strange man and his message had alarmed me. I wouldn't permit Mark to go hear him again. I shuddered at the thought of my only child becoming a follower of one who looked like a cave dweller, and sounded like an Old Testament prophet. My husband "Philip" had been an open-minded, modern Greek, but I was sure he would not have wanted his son Mark to become like John the Baptist.

The day we went looking for Jesus was one time I didn't have to hurry Mark to finish his lessons with his Greek tutor. By the time my personal servant Rhoda and I were ready to leave, Mark was waiting for us in the front courtyard with the servants who were carrying our provisions and several small sun tents.

His tutor was also waiting in the courtyard to go with us. I knew the tutor had his eye on Rhoda, the pretty young girl I had recently rescued from a cruel life. But so far, I had pretended not to notice his frequent glances her way. Besides, for that outing I welcomed the tutor's intelligent company for Mark.

In the afternoon, we found Jesus in the town of Bethany, which is about two miles from Jerusalem in the direction towards Jericho. Jesus was teaching and healing outside the home of the former leper, Simon the Pharisee, who was now back home with his wife Martha and her sister Mary and brother Lazarus.

At our synagogue, I had heard the good news about Simon's healing along with nine other lepers, but didn't realize Jesus was the healer. I think the moment I made that connection was the moment I believed in Jesus. And soon so did Mark and his tutor, as well as Rhoda and many others in my household.

For several days, we stayed in Bethany to be near Jesus. Before we headed back to Jerusalem, I invited Jesus and his disciples to stay in my home whenever they needed accommodations in Jerusalem. I told Judas, the group's business manager, I had dozens of sleeping pallets for guests.

I couldn't wait to tell Barnabas all that I had found out about Jesus. You know, I'm glad I didn't know then what was to come. My faith was new, and I needed time to grow strong in the Spirit. I needed to learn so much more from Jesus himself.

Decades later when God inspired my son Mark to write his Gospel, I was no longer alive on earth. Nor were most of us from that Bethany group – including Rhoda who became like a daughter to me and married Mark's tutor when she was of age. But whether we died by martyrdom or otherwise, our testimonies of the early days of Christianity lived on – both in historical tradition and in the New Testament.

Perhaps you'd like to know the verses dearest to me in the Gospel that Mark wrote after his missionary journeys with his Uncle Barnabas and Apostles Paul and Peter. These verses are ones you may not have noticed before. They tell about Mark's frightening experience at the time of Jesus' arrest.

These are his words: "*Then all the disciples forsook Jesus and fled. But a certain young man followed Jesus, having a linen cloth thrown around his naked body. And the men also laid hold of him, but he left the linen cloth and fled from them naked.*"

Did you notice? Even though he was but a teenager, Mark had more courage than many of the others. How proud his father would have been of him that night.

Mark fled back to the villa of "Judith" and Joseph of Arimathea where we women were still tidying up from the Lord's last Passover meal. Mark hurriedly wrapped himself in a borrowed cloak, and rushed with us to where Jesus was first taken that dreadful night.

Now do you still question where we women were during the Last Supper?

How could we not have served the meal that Passover night as we had countless other meals? Women like myself and Rhoda, Jesus' mother Mary and her sister Salome, "Naomi" who was healed of a twelve-year hemorrhage, Martha and Mary of Bethany, the wife of Simon Peter, Mary of Magdala, the "twins" Joanna and Susanna, and "Judith" whose upper family room we were in that night.

In fact, various ancient artworks of the Last Supper portray us there. For good reason, we just weren't there in Leonardo da Vinci's celebrated painting – the mural on the wall of the monastery dining hall in Milan that has dominated the perception of Christians for far too long.

But there's another time we women were there for the Master that no one dares question. It's too well documented, both in Biblical and historical accounts. We were there when Jesus was tried, and throughout the horrendous ordeal of his crucifixion and burial. Our sorrow was immense as we witnessed the Lord's unspeakable anguish. Because we did not flee as did some of his other disciples, we have often been referred to as the "women of the cross."

Standing in view of the cross on that dreadful, first Good Friday, how devastated we were. But how quickly our weeping changed to joy on the first Easter – that glorious morning we discovered Jesus was alive again.

"He's alive! He's alive!" we shouted, hurrying to tell his other followers hiding throughout Jerusalem since his death.

Several months later, my servant Rhoda shouted the same words again about the disciple Jesus called the Rock.

"He's alive! He's alive!" she shouted. "Peter's alive and standing at the gate!"

In her excitement that fateful night, Rhoda rushed back inside and left Peter locked outside. We were praying for courage for Peter and ourselves as we faced persecution and death. Never did we expect Peter to be miraculously released alive from prison by the Lord's angel.

Had Jesus been there, I expect he would have said: *"Oh, ye of little faith."*

For all of us, that night was a great lesson in God's almighty power. We realized not all of us would die soon for our faith. The Kingdom of Heaven on earth would become greater and endure longer than any of us had dreamed. And so I decided to leave Jerusalem and go to my family's villa in Rome as my brother Barnabas had been urging me to do.

From that time on, I gave my resources to further the Kingdom. I even encouraged my son Mark to become a weirdo if need be to fulfill Jesus' Great Commission. Remember those last words of Jesus to us? *"Go ye into all the world and preach the Gospel to every creature."*

* * *

Indeed, I, Mary, the mother of John Mark and the owner of Rhoda, was an ordinary person transformed by the power of Jesus Christ.

You, too, can experience this transformation, and live or die for the glory of God.

Amen and Amen.

Meditation Passages:
Acts 12:12; Colossians 4:10.

Chapter 10

Women of the Last Supper: "We Were There Too"

An Abridged Presentation

Authors's Note: This is an abridged presentation of the preceding nine chapters and can be presented in a single performance.

When you read the Gospels carefully, you will note that many women were with Jesus just before his last Passover supper with his twelve disciples. And we were there right after the Last Supper, and all throughout the dreadful events that followed.

So where were we women disciples during the Last Supper?

Don't you suppose we were there with Jesus then too? Don't you suppose we prepared the Passover and served it as we had countless other meals?

Of course, we were there, as various ancient artworks in Europe of the Last Supper portray so magnificently. We just weren't there in Leonardo da Vinci's famous mural in Milan – the painting on the wall of a monastery dining hall (a good reason not to include women), the one that has dominated the perception of so many for so long, especially in America.

The monologs that follow tell the stories of a few of us women disciples of Jesus in our own words. May you be blessed by our stories and drawn closer to Jesus.

Mary: A Mother Blessed

I am Mary of Nazareth – the mother of Jesus Christ, and one his close followers present at the Last Supper. Yes, I was a mother uniquely blessed – but also one acquainted with deepest grief.

My soul still magnifies the Lord when I recall the extraordinary events of my life. For whoever would have thought Yahweh would choose someone from Nazareth to bring into the world the Messiah – our Savior Jesus Christ, Redeemer of the World!

Joseph's family and mine were from the Tribe of Judah and descendants of the royal line of David. Had we lived before the terrible wars and captivities of the Jewish people, you would remember us as

Prince Joseph and Princess Mary. Ponder that a moment – makes the title *Prince of Peace* for my son Jesus more meaningful, doesn't it?

As you might expect, I was one of his closest followers – and one of his first women disciples. Yes, Jesus had his circle of twelve men disciples. But as the Holy Gospels state, there were many others who were also his disciples, including numerous women.

Among Jesus' women disciples were my sister Salome and myself, the sisters Mary and Martha from Bethany, Mary Magdalene, the wife of Simon Peter whose name history has lost, Mary the mother of John Mark and her servant Rhoda, "Naomi" whose twelve-year hemorrhage Jesus healed, the "twins" Joanna and Susanna, and my Aunt "Judith" who was the wife of Uncle Joseph of Arimathea.

Indeed, I, Mary, the blessed mother of our Lord and one of his woman disciples, was an ordinary person transformed by the power of Jesus Christ.

Salome: A Privileged Aunt

I am Salome – the sister of Jesus' mother Mary, and one of Jesus' close followers present at the

Last Supper. Since Jesus was my nephew, I was indeed a privileged aunt.

As you may recall from Biblical and historical records, before my marriage I was from Nazareth, located in the southern part of the province of Galilee. In Aramaic, Nazareth means "watchtower," a fitting name for my hometown that overlooked an important highway, and was frequented by trade caravans and Roman troops. Because traders and soldiers often camped in our community during their travels, other Jews liked to joke, "Can anything good come out of Nazareth?"

My nephew Jesus certainly changed that perception, didn't he?

In those days, we didn't know what the future held. But we did know Jesus was somehow special, and that whatever became of him would affect us all. If he really became the King of the Jews, as we increasingly hoped he would, I looked forward to my sons being right there beside him, serving as his closest advisers. I even mentioned to Mary a couple of times how I liked to imagine the three of them grown up and dressed in royal robes, ruling over a peaceful and prosperous kingdom together.

She would look off into the distance as she replied, "Well, you know, Salome, God's ways are often not our ways. But I hope whatever happens, our families will always be there for each other."

And we were.

Yes, Mary was right all those years ago when she quietly and repeatedly reminded me that God's ways are often not our ways. I learned that regardless of what happens, being a follower of Christ is the best way to live – even when doing so leads to persecution, loss of wealth, or death. There is no way to adequately describe God's amazing grace through Jesus Christ. It can only be experienced.

No, I will never regret that my family and I followed Christ, and that we provided from our abundance for his ministry here on earth.

Indeed, I, Salome, privileged to be the aunt of our Lord and Master, was an ordinary person transformed by the power of Jesus Christ – as were my sons James and John, along many others in our family.

"Naomi": An Outcast No Longer

I am "Naomi" – and like my namesake in the Old Testament, Yahweh turned my bitter lot in life to joy. From the moment of Jesus' amazing miracle in my life, no longer was I an outcast. In gratitude, I became one of his close followers and providers. How then, I ask, could anyone doubt my presence at the Last Supper?

But first, perhaps you'd like to know who I am and why I once was an outcast.

Gladly will I tell you my story. For my greatest joy, as the meaning of my name suggests, is sharing how I was instantly healed by Jesus – especially when my testimony brings faith and hope to others who suffer or doubt.

Ah yes, for many years I had sought healing. My life of bitterness began after my last child was born and my issue of blood did not cease. Not severe enough to end my life, my hemorrhage became my shame. For I was ceremonially unclean as long as I hemorrhaged. Mine was a family that carefully observed the Law, so I was isolated – an outcast in my own home, kept apart even from my loved ones.

If you've read my story in the Gospels, you know my healing was instant the moment I touched Jesus' cloak. Perhaps you remember as well that in the days to follow, hundreds more did as I. They also were instantly healed.

The moment I was healed, I felt clean and strong again, feelings I had long forgotten. Joy filled my whole being. I wanted to hug Jesus and everyone around him. I wanted to sing out, "I am whole. I am clean. I'm restored. No longer am I an outcast."

Naturally, I didn't expect Jesus to notice me. But he did. And because he noticed, in a few minutes my fear and shame were gone forever. I could indeed sing aloud and dance in front of everyone. Ah yes, the joy of that day fills me still, and I'm sure there's no need for me to describe my welcome home that evening.

With arms around my beloved family, I repeated for them Jesus' wonderful words: *"Daughter, be of good cheer; your faith has made you well. Go home in peace."*

From then on, I was one of the women who followed the Master. I knew what I gave to Jesus' ministry from my husband's wealth could never repay God for our new life. But at least my family and I were saying, "Thank you, Lord. Thank you."

The words Jesus said to Jairus and me that day so long ago, he still says: "*Don't be afraid; just believe.*" Yes, Jesus' amazing grace will be with each of you through whatever valleys your walks of faith may lead. Of that, I am proof.

Indeed, I, "Naomi," whose life was changed from bitterness to abundant joy, was an ordinary person transformed by the power of Jesus Christ.

Mary the Magdalene: An Early Church Leader

I am Mary of Magdala – one of history's most controversial women, and one of Jesus Christ's women disciples present at the Last Supper.

I urge you to be careful what you read and assume about me, for there are many religious scholars as well as others who seek to discredit both the Master and me. Unfortunately, their speculations overlook definite clues about me in the Gospels.

But fortunately, the most significant event of my life is clearly recorded in the Bible and cannot be misunderstood – I was the first witness of our resurrected Lord. Isn't that amazing affirmation for women of all time, everywhere?

Because I was the first to speak with Jesus after his resurrection and then to tell the good news to his disciples, I was known in the early years of the Church as "an apostle to the apostles." Some even called me the "thirteenth apostle." That was before much of my life's story became hidden and then forgotten.

Though I was a woman of independent means and with aristocratic status, until Jesus healed me, I suffered from a physical problem not even the best physicians could cure. I lived a life of privilege, yes, but my life was not normal, nor happy. For from time to time, demons seized me, tormented my body and threw me writhing and moaning to the ground.

During my times free of seizures, I lived a scholar's life. What else could I do? I certainly couldn't marry and have a family. So I studied religion, language, philosophy, history and more. Some of our family friends thought that was why demons came upon me, but we scoffed at that. In my family, females had long been given the advantages of learning, especially those of us blessed with good minds.

In fact, did you know that my scholarly interests are the reason Oxford and Cambridge Universities have colleges named after me? Ironic, isn't it, that for centuries after their founding, those colleges were for males only.

So you can see, when my time came to be a leader among Jesus' followers and in the early Church, I was ready. I eagerly used my abilities and inheritance for the Master. I was thrilled, as the Scriptures say, to be one of "*certain women who provided for Him from their substance.*" It was one way I could show my gratitude to the Lord for casting away my demons, and for revealing Yahweh, God of truth and light, to me. Furthermore, I wanted to make it possible for others, especially women, to find the spiritual joy and peace Jesus freely offers to those who follow him.

Following Jesus in person – those were the most wonderful three years of my life. And for the rest of my days, I never tired of telling the stories of Jesus to whoever would listen, especially to women and children.

I loved to tell about the Master's miracles – and there were far, far more than the few recorded in the Gospels.

Indeed, I, Mary of Magdala and a woman disciple of the Master, was an ordinary person transformed by the power of Jesus Christ.

"Judith": Wife of Joseph of Arimathea

I am "Judith" of Arimathea – the wife of Joseph the merchant who was a Jewish leader. And I am one of Jesus Christ's close followers present at the Last Supper.

Scarcely any records remain to tell my story, just a brief comment on my wifely status in the scrolls of the ancient historian Josephus. For as you know, in former days what women achieved was rarely recorded. That's one reason many of us excitedly followed Jesus – he cared about the experiences of women.

But the most important reason we followed him was because he reached our hearts with true spiritual love. We could sense his closeness to Yahweh, and his wisdom about life.

During the calm months of the year, Joseph and I often journeyed aboard one of our merchant ships to different Mediterranean ports. One summer, that's what we were doing when a freak, violent storm arose. I was terrified! I had never seen the sea so turbulent! I feared at any moment our ship might sink.

On that journey, we happened to have along several young relatives to keep our own children company. One of these was Joseph's great-nephew, the teenager Jesus of Nazareth. In those days, we didn't fully realize who he was, nor the extent of his powers. To our amazement, he didn't get seasick or frightened when the fierce storm threatened our lives and drove our ship off course.

In fact, he came to us and suggested with gentle authority, "Uncle Joseph and Aunt Judith, we've been blown close to a strange land. A sheltered cove lies a short ways to the north where we can drop anchor until the storm passes. Command the sailors to cease struggling against the gales, and let the ship be taken to where we will not be harmed."

Back then we didn't know the name of the place, but in a few minutes we had miraculously reached the coast of what you now call England, near Glastonbury. Years later, we remembered the cove when we had to flee for our lives. So that idyllic spot became not just a temporary refuge for us, but also our last home on earth. Interestingly, living there eventually connected us to the marvelous King Arthur tradition of Great Britain.

How could we have known then that the chalice we brought with us because the Master used it during his last Passover supper would become the Holy Grail? Or that this Holy Grail would be an inspiration to millions of Christians throughout the centuries?

Some may say it cost us too much to follow the Master. But we say, look how God provided a new home for us, and led us to people eager to hear about Christ and follow his true ways.

Should you travel today to Glastonbury, you can still visit places dear to us and hear the stories of miracles that happened. But the Holy Grail – is it there? Ah, dear friends, I know where it is, but I can't tell you. For God doesn't want you to follow the

Grail, but rather the way of the risen Christ it mysteriously represents.

Indeed, I, "Judith," wife of Joseph of Arimathea and a woman disciple of the Master, was an ordinary person transformed by the power of Jesus Christ.

An Unnamed Woman: the Wife of Simon Peter

I am an unnamed woman from Capernaum – the wife of Simon Peter, and one of Jesus Christ's women disciples present at the Last Supper.

Unnamed as I am in Biblical and historical records, be assured my name is written in the *Lamb's Book of Life*. For I was a close follower of God's Lamb, the Messiah of the world. And that's all that really matters, isn't it!

Though I am not named in the Gospels, nor even by the Apostle Paul when he mentioned to the Corinthians my travels with my husband Peter, the most important events of my life were recorded – of which the most important was living for the Master. But dying for his sake came next.

Perhaps you already know I was crucified along with Peter in Rome in 61 A.D. Side by side, we had served the Master throughout our lives. And for his sake, side by side we were martyred.

Thinking they could break Peter by making him witness my crucifixion, I was nailed on my cross first. But those ungodly, brutal Roman soldiers didn't know Peter. He was a true "rock" for the Master's Church. And they didn't know me. Above all, they didn't know the powerful grace of our Lord that sustains his followers in their times of greatest need.

On our crosses, Peter, who was upside down, gasped to me again and again, *"Remember the Lord!"* And I cried back to him those words of the martyrs. As we remembered the Lord's sacrifice for us, we were filled with grace to die for our Savior's sake. In spite of our agony, we did not deny Christ, nor did we betray our Christian sisters and brothers.

Yes, because we followed the Master, Peter and I lived extraordinary lives. Some would say the circumstances of our lives were fearsome. I agree. Some would say adventuresome. I agree. Some would say unbelievable. Again I agree. And some would say our lives were blessed. The last analysis is the best.

Indeed, I, the unnamed wife of Simon Peter and a woman disciple of the Master, was an ordinary person transformed by the power of Jesus Christ.

Martha: the Sister of Mary from Bethany

I am Martha of Bethany – the sister of Mary and Lazarus, and one of Jesus Christ's close followers present at the Last Supper. If you think of the Gospel accounts of my meal serving, who more fitting than I to be there!

Those who read carefully the passages from the Gospels telling about Mary, Lazarus and me, find that Simon, a healed leper, was from our same home in Bethany. Of course, for he was my husband and the source of our wealth At least, that's what some Bible scholars think. I'd also like to suggest to you that he was one of the ten lepers Jesus healed in the Gospel accounts – the one that returned to say "thank you." From that time on, he and I, Lazarus and Mary were all close followers of the Master.

Whatever you may have heard, my sister Mary was not a woman of the streets. But yes, she was an adulteress. She loved a man who would not marry her because his family objected. There were other men who wanted to marry her, for she was lovely in looks and person, and had a generous dowry. But Mary always said she would never marry a man she didn't love. A woman with money can say those words. So in that regard, she was fortunate. But in another regard, she was not. She only loved the one man, and so she never married.

Then Rabbi Jesus became our friend.

Because of his teachings, Mary's life was transformed. Soon, all she cared about were spiritual matters. The sins in her life were forgiven and she sinned no more. Remember Anna, the elderly prophetess who lived in the Temple? That's what Mary became – a woman dedicated to God because of His Son, Jesus Christ, our marvelous friend.

Alas, only a few hours after our Last Supper with this dear friend, one dreadful event after another happened. And many of us women disciples witnessed everything. Jesus had changed our lives! We couldn't let him suffer such agony alone. During his terrible ordeal, the words I said to him a short while before in Bethany kept coming back to me and giving me courage.

"Lord, I believe that you are the Christ, the Son of God," I had said. *"I believe you are the Messiah who is to come into the world. Lord, I believe. Lord, I believe."*

Indeed, I, Martha of Bethany and a woman disciple of the Master, was an ordinary person transformed by the power of Jesus Christ.

Joanna and Susanna: "Twin" Followers of Christ Memoir of Two Women Disciples

Joanna: Greetings in the name of our Lord, Jesus Christ. I am Joanna.

Susanna: And I am Susanna. We are "twin sisters" who were among Jesus' close women followers. Gladly did we follow Jesus, for he healed our infirmities and opened our hearts to his truth.

Joanna: Like some others who followed Jesus, I helped provide for our Lord and his group of closest followers. This I could do because I was the much-loved wife of a wealthy and generous Roman centurion.

Susanna: Yes, Joanna's husband Chuza was indeed generous, as well as kind. When my own husband Gaius was killed in a sword fight, my children and I were left in difficult circumstances, partly because of his gambling debts. My good brother-in-law was quick to suggest we live in his household. Since Joanna and I were often together in her home anyway, my children adjusted well to the change in our lives.

Joanna: We first met Jesus the day after he healed my husband Chuza's servant. Do you remember the Gospel account of that miracle just before Jesus brought the daughter of Jairus back to life?

Naturally, having something so wondrous happen in our household made all of us want to see and hear Jesus. We wanted to thank him for healing my husband's servant who had been with Chuza since his childhood and was like a dear uncle.

The day after the healing, many from our household went with us to the lakeshore to hear Jesus. We took along great quantities of provisions so we would have enough to share with Jesus and his close followers. Remember, there weren't any McDonald's or Pizza Huts back then.

At the end of that memorable day, both Susanna and I joined the other women disciples of Jesus. Chuza gave us his blessing to follow Jesus, and told us he would gladly help provide for Jesus ministry.

In the years that followed, Chuza brought the Good News of the Master to thousands of seekers before he was burned to death as one of Nero's torches in Rome. His last words to his loved ones were, "Fear not! Remember the Lord who is with us always!"

Indeed, we, Joanna and Susanna, "twin sisters" and married to Roman centurions, were among Jesus' close women followers. We were ordinary women transformed by the power of Jesus Christ.

You, too can experience this transformation, and live or die for the glory of God.

Mary: John Mark's Mother and Rhoda's Owner

I am Mary – the mother of John Marcus, or Mark as we usually called him. And I am the woman in whose home Rhoda was a servant. We three were among Jesus' close followers. As such, we were present at the Last Supper.

Living as we did in Jerusalem, we were active in the early Christian church. What amazing blessings from Yahweh we experienced! Gladly will I reveal to you now a little of my story.

Like some of the other women who followed Jesus, I helped provide for our Lord and his band of close followers. This I rejoiced to do, for I was a Jewish woman of independent means. I was the widow of "Philip" of Alexandria who came from a family of prominent Greek merchants.

That's how it happened our son Marcus, named for his paternal grandfather, was both Jew and Greek, not uncommon in Jerusalem during our time. So it was natural for Mark later in his life to move to Alexandria to establish the Christian church there and became its first bishop.

Even though I bear a famous name, I'm better known for my son Mark and my servant girl Rhoda than for myself. Their voices have been remembered in the Bible and by tradition far clearer than mine. But I wonder, would they have followed the Master if I had not done so first? Frightening, isn't it, to ponder the eternal effect of some of life's quickest choices! Daily I praise God that when it came to following Jesus, I made the right choice.

When God inspired my son Mark to write his Gospel, I was no longer alive on earth. Nor were most of us from that Bethany group – including Rhoda who became like a daughter to me and married Mark's tutor when she was of age. But whether we died by martyrdom or otherwise, our testimonies of the early days of Christianity lived on – both in historical tradition and in the New Testament.

Perhaps you'd like to know the verses dearest to me in the Gospel that Mark wrote after his missionary journeys with his Uncle Barnabas and Apostles Paul and Peter. These verses are ones you may not have noticed before. They tell about Mark's frightening experience at the time of Jesus' arrest.

These are his words: "*Then all the disciples forsook Jesus and fled. But a certain young man followed Jesus, having a linen cloth thrown around his naked body. And the men also laid hold of him, but he left the linen cloth and fled from them naked.*"

Did you notice? Even though he was but a teenager, Mark had more courage than many of the others. How proud his father would have been of him that night.

Mark fled back to the villa of "Judith" and Joseph of Arimathea where we women were still tidying up from the Lord's last Passover meal. Mark hurriedly wrapped himself in a borrowed cloak, and rushed with us to where Jesus was first taken that dreadful night.

Now do you still question where we women were <u>during</u> the Last Supper?

But there's another time we women were there for the Master that no one dares question. It's too well documented, both in Biblical and historical accounts. We were there when Jesus was tried, and throughout the horrendous ordeal of his crucifixion and burial. Our sorrow was immense as we witnessed the Lord's unspeakable anguish. Because we did not flee as did some of his other disciples, we have often been referred to as the "women of the cross."

Standing in view of the cross on that dreadful, first Good Friday, how devastated we were. But how quickly our weeping changed to joy on the first Easter – that glorious morning we discovered Jesus was alive again.

"He's alive! He's alive!" we shouted, hurrying to tell his other followers.

Indeed, I, Mary, the mother of John Mark and the owner of Rhoda, and all these others were ordinary persons transformed by the power of Jesus Christ.

You, too, can experience this transformation, and live or die for the glory of God. *Amen.*

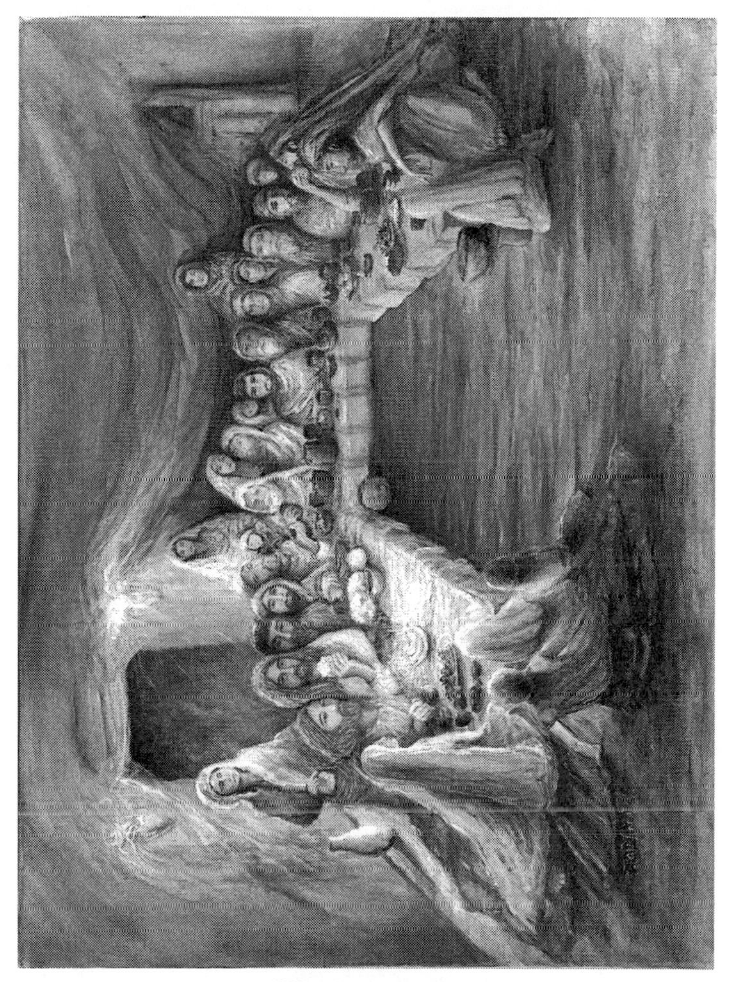

"The Invitation"
Artist Jan Von Bokel

Limited Edition of 100, 22" x 28"
Archival Giclee Canvas